Every Woman Wears A Crown

Verses of strength, grace and resilience

Wg Cdr Charu Sharma (Retd)

Copyright © Wg Cdr Charu Sharma (Retd)
All Rights Reserved.

This book has been self-published with all reasonable efforts taken to make the material error-free by the author. No part of this book shall be used, reproduced in any manner whatsoever without written permission from the author, except in the case of brief quotations embodied in critical articles and reviews.

The Author of this book is solely responsible and liable for its content including but not limited to the views, representations, descriptions, statements, information, opinions, and references ["Content"]. The Content of this book shall not constitute or be construed or deemed to reflect the opinion or expression of the Publisher or Editor. Neither the Publisher nor Editor endorse or approve the Content of this book or guarantee the reliability, accuracy, or completeness of the Content published herein and do not make any representations or warranties of any kind, express or implied, including but not limited to the implied warranties of merchantability, fitness for a particular purpose.

The Publisher and Editor shall not be liable whatsoever...

Made with ❤ on the BookLeaf Publishing Platform
www.bookleafpub.in
www.bookleafpub.com

Dedication

To every woman who has ever doubted her strength, questioned her worth or silenced her own voice - this book is for you. May you always remember that you wear a crown, not of gold or jewels, but of grace, resilience and the desire to grow.

To my mother, whose love and wisdom continue to guide me.

To all the women who inspire, uplift and empower - this is our story, our poetry and our crown!

Preface

"Every Woman Wears a Crown" is a celebration of the quiet strength, resilience and grace that define womanhood. Through these verses, I have attempted to capture the essence of the many roles a woman plays - daughter, mother, sister, friend, leader, dreamer and warrior.

This book is not just a collection of poetry - it is a tribute to every woman who has ever stood tall despite the storms, carried the weight of expectations with dignity and embraced her imperfections as part of her unique brilliance. Whether adorned in a uniform, a corporate suit, a saree or simply her own skin, she wears her crown with quiet confidence.

As you turn these pages, I hope you find echoes of your own journey, your own battles and your own triumphs. May these words remind you that no matter where you stand in life, your crown is yours alone—unshakable, irreplaceable and undeniably majestic.

With love and strength,
Charu

Acknowledgements

Writing this book has been a journey of self-discovery, emotions and empowerment. I am deeply grateful to BookLeaf Publishing for giving me this opportunity.

To the women who inspire these verses — mothers, daughters, sisters, friends, warriors in uniforms, sarees and suits. Thank you for reminding the world every day that a crown isn't always made of gold, but of grace, strength and resilience.

To my parents, for being the wind beneath my wings. You have always pushed me to achieve more, empowered me to dream fearlessly and chase those dreams while disregarding all the people who told them that daughters come with limitations.

To my family, especially my husband and children — your unwavering love and patience gave me the wings to write.

To my readers — may you find pieces of yourself in these pages and may each poem remind you of your worth, your voice and your crown.

And finally, to the girl I once was — unsure but curious, soft yet strong. Thank you for never giving up. This is your voice, your affirmation.

With gratitude and grace,
Charu

1. Every Woman Wears a Crown

She walks with grace, head held high,
Spark of fire in her eye.
They whisper doubts, to keep her bound,
With strength and resilience she stands her ground.

Through storms she stands, through pain she grows,
With every scar her radiance glows.
She lifts the fallen, wipes their tears,
With courage of conviction, defies her fears.

She's the mother, the daughter, the guiding light,
A spark of courage in the darkest night.
She needs no throne, no grand renown,
For every woman wears a crown.

Her crown is woven with threads of care,
In every sacrifice, she's there.
She nurtures, heals and dares to dream,
Carving her path with her own theme.

2. Echo of Doubts

I took a step, the ground felt weak,
The path ahead was dark and bleak.
Whispers followed sharp and cold,
”You can’t make it?”, I was told.

Doubt crept in, sometimes a tear,
Filling my mind with silent fear.
“What if they are right?”, my heart would say,
”What if I fail and lose my way?”.

Who are they to question my wings, my right to soar?
As if success has a bolted door!
The phoenix never took permission to rise,
The ones who made breakthroughs didn’t seek the
world’s advice.

I carved my own path, built my own throne,
Proved to myself what I had always known.
For doubts may scream, they hold no key,
The only limit for me, is set by me.

3. Rising in Solidarity

Not just one, but hand in hand,
Together as sisters, we take a stand.
Lifting each other, sharing the load,
Stronger we rise, when we honour the behen-code.

These are Indra Nooyi's words which fuel that feeling -
"The glass ceiling will go away when women help other
women break through that ceiling".
And when the ceiling shatters, the barriers explode,
Women are no longer questioned, no longer bestowed.

We are the storm, the flower, the flame,
No more whispers, no more shame.
No dream too bold, no path too steep,
With hearts as fierce as the goals we keep.

4. She's the Song

A woman of grace, with a spirit of sunshine,
Has golden hair with a voice divine.
With every note, she lifts the soul,
Spreading love and positivity is her goal.

With every word, with every glance,
She lifts up others, giving them a chance.
A hand to hold, a shoulder to lean,
Her heart is vast, strong and serene.

Her soul is a beacon of love and grace,
She helps, she smiles, she lights up the place.
A woman of strength, of power and might,
A queen in her own way, shining bright.

5. The Walls I Build

I build my walls, not out of spite,
But to guard my peace, my burning light.
A sacred space where I can breathe,
Without the weight of what others believe.

Not every call is meant for me,
Life has no limits, so let me be.
I choose the voices that bring me grace,
And walk away from a draining embrace.

So if I step back, you can understand,
I hold no malice, just take my stand.
For in these walls, my spirit stays free,
A place of peace, just meant for me.

We all need our space, free of insecurities,
Where we decide what's best for us, not authorities.
That's why we need to set boundaries,
For emotional health and mental peace.

6. Bring it On
(Inspired by Mrs Deepa Malik)

I met her once, her smile so sweet,
Her impact itself is a remarkable feat.
With strength in her heart and courage so deep,
She rose from the ashes, refusing to weep.

A Paralympian, she's fearless with medals in hand,
Her name etched in gold, across the land.
With strength beyond measure, she broke each chain,
Proving that limitations are only in the brain

"Disabilities?!" she says with a smile,
"Just hurdles to cross, I'll go that extra mile."
In every race, in every strife,
She's shown the world the power of life.

A warrior of the mind, a conqueror of dreams,
She teaches us hope, no matter how it seems.

Deeply inspired, I carry your light,
As I chase my dreams, through day and night.

7. Let's Talk

Let's talk, not in hushed whispers,
Not behind closed doors,
But out in the open,
Of the battles women silently endure.

Let's talk of the bruises hidden deep,
'Adjustments' she is required to keep.
They praise her strength for playing every role,
While freedom remains a distant goal.

Let's talk of bodies judged and shamed,
Choices stolen, then blamed.
Of clothes debated more than crimes,
Justice lost between the lines.

Let's talk about those women too,
Once bound, now holding on to the old view.
What she endured, she will sustain,
Rejoicing in the scars it leaves again.

Let's talk, not just on one day,
Not just in a hall or a play,
But in every home, to make a start,
With open minds and open heart.

8. Rest.Reflect.Rise

Take out some time, not for someone else,
To sit with the silence and find yourself.
A book, a walk, a song, a sigh,
Enjoy the moments, let the time fly.

Don't shrink to make others feel tall,
Nurture your growth, never let it stall.
Water the garden your soul has built,
Pamper yourself without any guilt.

Stay away from those who dim your light,
When their presence feels more wrong than right.
Don't let them drain you, break your peace,
The right ones will bring the right vibe of ease.

And when they ask you how you shine so bright,
Say that I chose myself every day, every night.
So take out some time, let your heart explore,
For in self-discovery, you'll find so much more.

9. Inheritance of Love

Not all wealth is made of gold,
It's in the warmth of memories, of stories told.
Some treasures don't reflect a shine,
They grow through bonds we call 'mine'.

She left too soon, my guiding light,
Taught me wisdom is in knowing to choose my fight.
Her love lingers, deep and true,
In all I am, in all I do.

I've inherited more than name or face,
More than rituals, roots or place.
She gave me grace in cups of tea,
And love that asked for nothing from me.

She taught me kindness without show,
To give, to rise, to simply glow.
Her lessons live in how I care,
In every quiet, unseen prayer.

Now it's my turn to give and grow,
To pass it down so that they know.
That love, not land, is the richest part,
True inheritance is the heart.

10. More Than Love

He is my calm, my storm, my spark,
The one who sees me in the dark.
My worst critic, sharp and true,
But only so I rise anew.

He holds the mirror to my face,
Then cheers the loudest in my race.
He pushes me, past every line,
Knows which battles must be mine.

He reads the thoughts I haven't said,
Knows all the storms inside my head.
He hears the silence in my voice,
And somehow makes the braver choice.

And more than all he gives to me,
He shows our kids the way to be.
That women aren't to just admire,
But to respect, empower and inspire.

11. Not a Mannequin

They whisper softly as she walks,
Their eyes judge first, before she talks.
They measure worth in shape and size,
Wanting her to shrink to fit their lies.

With love and pain, she's borne two souls,
Sacred scars, she's paid the tolls.
Her face is dull, she's lost her spark,
The world moved on, she missed her mark.

If they don't get you, don't bother!
Don't explain yourself to another.
Wear your confidence like gold,
Your beauty, your spirit cannot be controlled.
Wit and elegance is your shield,
Your self-respect shall never yield.

So let them talk and let them stare,
You're far too strong to even care.

Your worth is not for them to weigh,
Their opinions drift, then fade away.

12. Failure is Not Defeat

A queen is not made by flawless reign,
But by rising each time she walks through pain.
Yes, she stumbles, but does not fall,
She learns, she grows and she stands tall.

She's not afraid to miss the mark,
To chase her dreams through light and dark.
For every failure and every bruise,
She gathers strength and learns to choose.

Failure to her, is not defeat,
It's dust on the path beneath her feet.
A lesson dressed in rough disguise,
A quiet push toward greater skies.

She wears her scars like royal thread,
A crown of trials on her head.
She knows that greatness isn't fast,
It's built with grit, it's meant to last.

And so she walks, through doubt and flame,
A queen, unshaken, bold in name.
For she who's failed and dared again
Will always rise and always reign.

13. Lines of Life

Lines on her face, left behind,
Whispers of wisdom, gently aligned.
In every step, a lesson learned,
From bridges crossed to pages turned.
Of breaking glass and building walls,
Of holding space when no one calls.

Lines on her hands from trials she learnt to face
Of holding ground and finding place.
Of building dreams with silent might,
While lifting others into light.
The dreams she chased, the ones she shelved,
The versions of herself she held.

Lines on her spirit, forged in fire,
Reflecting the depths of her wild desire.
Of battles fought in silent grace,
And moments that time couldn't erase.
In every tear, a river flows,
In every laugh, a garden grows.

Some choose to hide these lines,
While others toast them with wines.
Both are strong, both are wise,
Their courage and grace no one denies.
No shame in age, no shame in skin,
Let self-love rise and always win.

So raise a glass to every line,
To paths once hidden, now brightly shine.
For in the beauty of each trace,
We find our strength, our sacred space.
A living testament, woven and vast,
In every line, we honor the past.

14. In a Man's World

In a man's world, breaking every chain,
She treads with courage, tackling the game.
In spaces crowded, where they dominate,
She fights for chances, they still hesitate.

Her hands are skilled but doubted,
With walls of bias, she's outed.
She doesn't drink, she doesn't smoke,
So opportunities slip, while she bears every misogynist
joke.

Her maternity calls are called frivolous,
Evoking guilt in her for exploiting a privilege.
No matter how much she works, how long she stays,
Her efforts still don't earn the praise.

It's never enough, though she gives her best,
Her worth still questioned, put to test.
And when she comes home, her heart in dismay,
She's asked, "What have you done all day?"

She's built her dreams, wore them with pride,
But still, there's judgment she can't hide.
For the world expects her to do it all,
Be the mother, the worker and answer duty's call.

But why must she stretch herself so thin,
When all she seeks is peace within.
Why burden herself with tasks so vast,
When motherhood's joy could be her path.

Deep within, there's something more,
A need for freedom, something to adore.
To stand on her own, with choices in hand,
Financially free, living her life the way she planned.

The world demands, but she seeks the key,
To shape her life with autonomy.
For though love and care are her heart's true choice,
She strives for power to speak with her voice.

15. Great Things Take Time

A seed won't bloom the day it's sown,
It needs the dark to grow alone.
The roots reach deep before the rise,
Beneath the soil, beneath the skies.

Ideas too, begin so small,
A flicker, hardly seen at all.
Feed them well with thought and grace,
And they will blossom in their place.

So give it time, don't force the pace,
Beauty lies in a slower race.
Let failure teach, let silence guide,
Let stillness be your trusted tide.

When storms arise and winds blow,
Rooted in faith, we learn to grow.
The journey weaves through light and dark,
With every stumble, we leave a mark.

16. In the Mirror, Me

I looked in the mirror and smiled today,
Not for how I looked, but for walking my way.
For rising from pieces I once swept aside,
For being the calm in my own rising tide.

I learned that rest is not being lazy,
That peace isn't selfish, it's just not crazy.
That "no" is a sentence, complete and strong,
That healing is slow and that's not wrong.

I forgive the girl who always gave in,
Who searched for worth in someone else's skin.
Today I choose her, stronger and true,
With all her flaws and all she's been through.

So here's to the mirrors, the truths we embrace,
To every tear that found its place.
To loving myself and knowing my worth,
A journey of healing, of joy and rebirth.

17. Sojourn

A fleeting stop on roads unplanned,
Life is a map of shifting sands,
We make a home in moments brief,
In laughter shared, in silent grief.

We step through doors that won't stay wide,
Meet souls who walk a while beside.
A conversation, brief and bright,
Can leave a mark, make your heart ignite.

This is a sojourn, not the end,
A bend, a phase, a time to mend.
We're shaped by every road we roam,
Including stops that never felt like home.

And yet, they carve into our core,
A version of us not there before.
And though the parting always comes,
The music lingers when it's done.

So learn to stay and then let go,
For life's transit, swift and slow.
Not because we're lost, but free,
Becoming who we're meant to be.

18. Before She Left

Before she left, she said it low,
With trembling voice, but steady glow.
I'm in love with who you used to be,
The man who once saw all of me.

You displayed chivalry, rare and sweet,
Wrote poetry, brought roses, swept me off my feet.
We danced through nights without regret,
And built a world I cannot forget.

But love, I've learned, is not the start,
A fire that flares, then falls apart.
It's in showing affection, day by day,
In words you choose, in what you say.

You showed me dreams, then gave me doubt,
Closed the door, then shut me out.
And still I stayed, because I knew,
The man you were, your shades of blue.

I've had enough, finished my search,
For love that leaves me in the lurch.
I won't keep begging to be seen,
No more illusions denying what has been.

This is not a bitter end,
Just me reclaiming what I defend.
My peace, my worth, my right to grow,
Even if it means letting you go.

19. Are We There Yet?

Just when you think we've crossed the line,
Shattered ceilings, our roles redefined.
A voice appears, sharp and sly,
Dressed in culture, wrapped in lie.

A quiet war, a daily test,
A million ways she must be less.
They call it tradition. She sees control.
They call her uncultured to justify the troll.

They preach respect, then mock her might,
They fear the way she claims her right.
Still she rises, cuts through noise,
Claims her place, her voice, her poise.

So, are we there yet? We have miles to go,
Still breaking chains while trying to grow.
But oh, the sting when progress bends,
By those who should be our allies, our friends.

20. Tea, Sunlight and Love

She did not need much,
Just respect, kindness, love and such.
Finding joy in nature, charm in mundane,
The scent of the earth, the sound of rain.

Clean water, fresh air,
Glowing skin and shiny voluminous hair.
A safe space where she can express,
Free from judgment, free from stress.

Books that carry away to distant lands,
A cup of tea, warm in her hands.
A garden kissed by dawn's first light,
Filled with flowers to soothe the sight.

The laughter of her children, a melody sweet,
A song of innocence, a peaceful retreat.
The company of friends, deep conversations,
Heartfelt moments with no explanations.

21. Why Don't You Like Me?

I enter your home with folded hands,
No hidden motives and no demands.
I haven't spoken with rage or spite,
I try my best to do what's right.

I didn't come here to steal your son,
To compete with you and say I've won.
Then why am I an outsider here,
When I traded my comfort and all that's dear?

I'm not a master of every chore,
I drop a spoon, step with slippers on the kitchen floor.
But my heart is trying every day,
To learn your world, to find a way.

You look at me with quiet scorn,
As if my presence makes you mourn.
As if I took, but never gave,
As if my worth is yours to waive.

I've achieved my dreams, my parents pride,
Yet in your home, I shrink, I hide.
Whatever i do is not enough,
Why is accepting me so tough?

I may not be perfect, not even close,
In your world of views i learn to pose.
I just want to live and to grow,
And offer love, if you'd let it show.

So tell me softly, if you can,
Why don't you like me? What's the plan?
For I came here not to win or lose,
But to be treated like a daughter - just like you!

www.ingramcontent.com/pod-product-compliance
Lightning Source LLC
LaVergne TN
LVHW010022200726
843495LV00015B/1875